Words without Sound

Davie White

Words without Sound

Copyright Page

Table of Contents

Dedication

Mom, I dedicate your book of poetry to you. As your daughter and publisher, it is an honor to present to you, your gift which you have composed. My prayer is that the presentation of your book will inspire you, as well as others, to love, dream, and believe again!

With lots of love,

Armani W.

Introduction

Love is something we all strive towards. However, what happens when two lovers love until the end of themselves? What happens when love seems to be attainable, yet still so far away? What happens when Him and Her confront each other about the love they have shared?

Will they fight for the love they cherish so profoundly? Or walk away as if the love they have shared, had never been?

Words without Sound is an expression of love shared through painful experiences at times. It is the heart's cry between two lovers who are desperately trying to figure love out. They have been through everything together. Yet, as Her finds herself, the two lovers are faced with crossroads. What will they do? How will love react?

Journey with Him and Her as they begin to unravel their idea and perception of love and the love they have for one another. Buckle your seatbelt, and hop on for a ride; a ride that only Words without Sound can provide!

My Fabulous Lover

Who knew we'd share a love like yours and mine?

A love that grew to be fabulous with the test of time!

I said in my heart, 'she's the right one, the right one for me!

I know because she loves me fabulously!"

"You see, she gives me her love, so abundantly;

And when I'm on the computer, she flirts with me!

No man, no riches can pay for what she gives!

If you don't have what I have, well then, you've never lived!

She's well-kept, well-groomed, and her smile brightens up any room!

I can't quite put my finger on it, maybe it's her aura!

But, I know this much, I'm in love with her, and yes, I adore her!

She keeps my physical and mental in check!

And gives me peace of mind, like no one I've ever met!

She believes in me and represents her man 100 percent

And she doesn't mind putting him first , that's just how she represents!

Damn, it feels great, when a man finds his helpmate!

It's been 17 years, and it's not hard for me to love her!

And I'm not tired yet, I'm still doing push-ups for her!

When I close my eyes, I can visualize when we first met

Damn, I said to myself, what a prize!

Hair in a ponytail, yeah, she wears it well!

I love the way she enjoys my company;

So completely and carefree!

And she's totally committed to me!

Yeah, that's my Davie! Fierce, resourceful and filled with ingenuity!

From Him —

The Hard Card

I'm looking for my soul mate

Because I want to create a happy home;

I no longer want to roam

the street or beat my meat,

I get hard every time I meet

A fine chick with a slick attitude

Towards any dude – who sells her

Hopes and a dream

Of being his Queen!

But they cause a scene

When I wanna leave

Every time I roll up my sleeve

To make a buck on my truck!

Relationships suck, but I need

To fuck only one woman,

But it seems too hard to choose

'Cause I can't lose my appetite

For every woman in my sight!

It's not my fault that God did

Such a great job!

Damn! All He did was make mine hard!

But, a playa's gotta play his card!

From Him —

Finding your Soul mate

Don't look for your soul mate,

Love your mate with all of your soul,

For this reason, God made two become whole!

To give meaning to your life

Between a husband and his wife!

Not for you to waste your time

Searching for a love you cannot find!

Not from the outside in, but from the inside out!

For when you love someone from deep within

It removes all doubt!

Therefore, you no longer have to wonder,

Whom God has placed together;

Let NO MAN put asunder!

From Her —

Chasing Women

You dog around town

Chasing women around

Knowing good and well,

Tomorrow you'll be wearing a frown

Like it's going out of style!

Just because the whole while;

You wanted to puff up your chest and profile!

Lying, saying , my only dream is to make her smile!

Thinking you're a Don or a King!

Don't you know that makes your

Ring don't mean a thing!

What good is your treasure

If you have nothing to measure?

Except you sold your soul for pleasure!

Now you walk around begging

And paying every woman in town

To spend just a little time with you!

Asking them would they like to

Go to a movie and maybe dinner, too!

Knowing deep down inside;

You just want to ball up and cry!

Because you don't want to let down your pride!

Or the lust you have in your eye!

Instead you would trade in love for lies

Not knowing you artistically caused

That love to die!

How powerful a thing of you to do

To set it up, so love could never return to you!

Destruction that comes from the hand of someone

Who calls himself a man!

Instead of standing on a rock;

You choose to sink in quick-sand!

Don't you know I was your greatest fan!

Cheering you on, believing you can

Take over the world and build us a home

On fertile land!

How can you be trusted?

Even though you shower you're still busted!

Leaving me disgusted; with a bitter taste

In my mouth, because I feel so disgusted!

Repulsed, I regurgitate all the hate

Your hands did create!

I marvel in wonder and surprise

To see the great length you go

To sell and tell your lies!

But to find the truth in you is so far away!

And for the truth you don't budge, you just sit and you stay!

I scratch my head and shake it in shame!

And shutter at the thought of almost taking your name!

No! since I've allowed myself to succumb to a man like you

My life has never been the same!

I take back my dignity

And move forward in Victory!

From Her —

The Comeback Attack

Why criticize me for my lies?

Don't you realize, my game, you can't despise!

It helps you to disguise your pitiful life!

Before me, there was no you!

I made you who you are today!

You've got a brand-new strut and you're even starting to sway!

Your girlfriends look at you filled with envy!

Because they wish they could be like you;

And have a man like me!

Without me there is no you!

When I met you, you were nothing but a ghetto bitch,

Now you're walking around with a twitch!

'Cause you got an itch that only I can fix!

A fixation that causes devastation!

And now you walk around with an attitude

Because you can't feel the magnitude of my pulsation!

But you beg me to give you my creation!

But my seed didn't succeed, it only made you bleed!

But I refused to feed you the love you think you need!

You got your hand out, asking for your allowance!

Hoping and praying, I'd give you a pence!

Girl, that just don't make no sense!

'Cause you keep walking away!

And you got the nerve to say,

I'm just wasting my time,

When I've already made money for the day!

I'm a clever predator, lying up in the cut!

Seeking whom I can devour,

When I shower you with gifts and flowers!

You have what most women only hope for!

Why would you dare to expect more?

You put your nose in the air,

Like you're so much better than me!

Or like I can't see!

That you're just like everyone else, you come with a price!

But, baby, I've already been there

More than once or twice!

You try to fight it and you try to hide it!

But deep down inside, I stripped you of all your pride!

You say you're looking for a man,

You know that's not true!

You're just looking for a taste, because I am a man

And I'm staring right in your face!

I tried to love you and save you from disgrace,

But after a while, I just realized

You're nothing but a hopeless case!

I tried to call you on the phone

And talk to you like a queen!

But you just spit out poisonous venom

And you treated me mean!

You say you wanna hear the truth

And I tell you I love you in so many ways!

But, baby, I just can't think of nothing else to say,

You've got my mind in a daze!

Girl, you so crazy! Let's stop all this fighting and arguing!

Come back into my arms, I promise I'll never harm you again!

I never meant to hurt you

'Cause when I hurt you, baby, I hurt me too!

I close my eyes tight, when I think of losing you!

The girls just gave me exposure, because

I couldn't gain my composure!

I can rip a bear apart, I can run a business night or day,

But I just can't figure you out and that's a damn shame

Because you know you've got my heart!

Baby, don't run away from us!

Don't tear us apart!

We've spent so much time,

You were Bonnie and I was Clyde!

I can't just say goodbye to all those good times.

Remember your birthdays, Christmas and New Year's

How we smiled together, and kept warm in the cold weather?

Girl, I even gave you my sweater!

When I look at your pictures, your smile is so sweet!

I get chills all through me and my legs get weak!

I try to reach out to you, I feel you slipping so far away!

You're out of my grasp, when I want you to stay!

Even though I front, like I no longer want you,

I know deep in my heart, no one can replace you!

But, here's one last thing I have to say to you!

As the stars in the sky, are way up high;

Look up at the moon, because I'm still

In my pushed up position, and I'll be back, soon!

Then when I'm finished with you,

I'm moving on to the next woman, too!

From Him —

Davie White

Text Love

Every time I get your text;

I wonder what's the next

Trick you've got up your sleeve

To make me say, please don't leave!

But, I'm tired and we're through

I can't take no more; I'm telling you!

I wanna just walk away,

You'll always remain the same

With all your childish games

That drive me insane!

I feel the need to break this chain

Of the bond between us!

I want to go quietly without a fuss,

But, you want to argue and cuss!

To get my attention with accusations

That only causes frustration!

You lie about the devastation of losing me!

Because you seem really happy

From what I can see!

From Her —

Why do you Hack Like That?

Yeah, yeah, yea, and all that Jazz!

You keep talking that Razz-z-ma-tazz!

I can see in your eyes, you're hypnotized,

But not only that, it's the way you open up your thighs,

And how you moan when I'm inside!

You think I don't have a clue of what you're up to!

Acting like you walked away without taking another look

Knowing good and well you hacked into my Facebook!

Every time I log onto AOL, I can tell

You've been creeping and spying but you're

Just not woman enough, to tell me,

'Baby, I want you back!' instead you read my messages,

You'd rather hack!

What you found made you cry,

But that message wasn't meant for your eyes!

She's more woman than you could ever be,

You're just a little girl to me, and you can't see

That together, we could've made History!

Yeah, I said it, I didn't stutter!

That thought of me being with another woman makes you shutter!

Now I feel like a louse, 'cause you got me in the doghouse!

And you no longer wish to be my spouse!

But, you'll never find another man with a master plan

To be the greatest that God created!

From Him —

I Got Dreams, I Swear!

I got dreams of owning my own day care!

But I swear, it feels like I ain't getting nowhere!

Because it's evident you want to make me co-dependent!

You pretend and you divert my attention

On all the gifts you make mention of!

Just so you can feel like you're above!

Thinking you can buy my love!

Love comes from the heart!

That's why you can't finish what you start!

Even a child can see, that's just crazy!

You tell me, you love me,

But that's just words without a sound

To keep me around, and to pull me down!

I got dreams, I swear!

I can hear the Lord calling me from up above

But His voice is so faint,

because I'm too wrapped up in my love!

How could I lose my focus,

His lies of holding me down seem so bogus

I thought it would be the two of us,

But he just wants to diminish me, and deem me unworthy!

But I know I've got values, because, I've got dreams, too!

I got dreams, I swear, but being with him,

I feel like I ain't getting nowhere!

From Her —

My Rabbit's Got a Habit

You say you want a day care

And your dreams, I do not share!

But you hop around like a bunny rabbit

And you ain't getting nowhere!

Now, you want me to disappear,

But, baby, look, open your eyes, I'm still here!

Right by your side,

Right or wrong, where I belong!

I took off from work just to take a long ride,

I wanted to give you a great surprise!

But route 78, I decided to hide!

I came to help you get started,

But you shewed me away and we parted!

You've got to be kidding me!

How could this be true!

I've driven more than four states for you!

And now it's your fault, you costed me $700

I wasn't with her, she lied and she fronted!

I was at my mother's house in Queens!

Now, I'm here with you to help you build your dreams!

I left my phone in the car, and it was turned off

What are you questioning me like that for?

You're lucky to see me, because any woman would be thrilled with chills

I wanted to surprise, but surprise, surprise,

There's nothing here, but a basket full of lies!

I worked on my mom's furnace and had to jet,

So I took a shower, because I didn't want you to smell my sweat!

Davie White

I keep a gym bag in my car

Just in case I have to travel far!

You said you called her, and she told you differently!

Yeah right, and I bet you she said there were three!

Damn girl, this is crazy, it's a shame!

I wasn't with her, you're just insane!

Let's stop playing these games

And get back to being the same,

So I don't want to hear you repeating her name!

She's just a friend, and I wanted to keep her

Close to me to see if we could go deeper

But I have no interest in being more

Than what she and I were meant for!

I can't pretend, she's just my friend!

Okay, I lied, it was her house instead,

Let's just move on with our lives, before our love goes
dead

You'll never get anywhere and you'll never find another
man with a love like mine!

If you leave, I swear your entire house will fall

You can't stand on your own, you're just not that tall!

For this kind of man, you're just too small!

And you'll only end up regretting it all!

From Him —

My Magician on a Mission

You say I'm a rabbit with a habit

But you're just a magician on a mission

You give me your gifts

With strings attached

And if I don't dance to the tune of your beat

You set me up for defeat

And magically your gifts, just disappear

It seems like a miracle right into thin air

You have this look on your face, like you just don't care

Then you lie, and you swear that for me you're here

You say you're a rarity, but you create destruction and disparity!

You destroy everything you touch, after you get me to trust!

You act like you've got the golden touch,

But everything you touch turns into rust!

You claimed you wanted to give me the world,

When in reality, you just wanted me to act like a squirrel.

You only created a false sense of security

Pretending like we shared chemistry

Pretending like you're a man of good quality

Say what you mean, and mean what you say,

Instead of lying and preaching false doctrine that way!

A wayward man is unstable in every way

And as the wind blows is where he will stray!

You think just because I've got gratitude,

That you have the right to present yourself

To me like a grimy dude!

Then you say I've got an attitude, and I'm acting rude!

Playing mind games, is just cruel

But I understand, you can't take the weight of your responsibility, so you happily shun it on me!

Don't even try it, go on a diet, 'cause I just don't buy it!

Expensive perfumes, and hotel rooms

So it's okay, you just assume

I'd go for any lie, if I want to keep you

I'd close my eyes!

Keep my mouth shut tight, for my own good!

I'm just crazy, and I misunderstood

Your intention, I'm crazy and demented

Lying to me, is not what you intended!

I get it, I see, I'm just digging my own grave,

But I'd rather do that than to be your slave!

You glorify yourself, and puff yourself up

Then you pretend to be humble, and you've still got the strut

Of a man filled with arrogance and misrepresentation

Saying you're the victim is your favorite proclamation!

The longer I stay, the further away

I'll continue to be from my victory!

You create such an air of hostility!

You have no shame or humility!

Playing one against the other!

How can we ever become united and just love one another?

I want to be free to love and free to live

Free to breath and free to give!

Lie after lie, after lie, after lie!

I can't listen anymore, it's just a disguise!

It's too much for my ears to hear,

Davie White

I can't take it anymore, I've cried my last tear!

Be the magic man that you are,

And just disappear!

From Her —

The end of a love affair, is the beginning to be becoming aware.

Find yourself, love yourself and pray to God that true love will follow

The End. The Beginning to Beginning